ART AND RELIGION IN ANCIENT GREECE

MELANIE ANN APEL

ROSEN CLASSROOM
PRIMARYSOURCE
Rosen Classroom Books & Materials

New York

To those who were brought together through the drama, despite the religion: My wonderful parents.
Love, Melanie

Published in 2004 by The Rosen Publishing Group, Inc.
29 East 21st Street, New York, NY 10010

First Edition

Editor: Joanne Randolph
Book Design: Michael de Guzman
Layout Design: Kim Sonsky
Photo Researcher: Peter Tomlinson

Photo Credits: Cover © David Lees/CORBIS; cover (bottom) Louvre, Paris, France/Peter Willi/Bridgeman Art Library; pp. 4 (top), 12 (left), 15 (bottom) © Erich Lessing/Art Resource, NY; p. 4 (bottom) The Art Archive/National Glyptothek Museum/Dagli Orti (A); p. 7 © Réunion des Musées Nationaux/Art Resource, NY; pp. 8, 11, 19 (top and center), 20 (bottom) The Art Archive/Dagli Orti; p. 11 (inset) © CORBIS; p. 12 (right) Staatliche Museum, Berlin, Germany/Bridgeman Art Library; pp. 15 (top and center), 16 (top) The Art Archive/National Archaeological Museum Athens/Dagli Orti; p. 16 (bottom) © Archivo Iconigrafico, S.A./CORBIS; p. 19 (bottom) The Art Archive/Archaeological Museum Piraeus/Dagli Orti; p. 20 (top) The Art Archive/British Museum/Eileen Tweedy, p. 20 (left) © The British Museum.

Apel, Melanie Ann.
Art and religion in ancient Greece/Melanie Ann Apel. - 1st ed.
p. cm.—(Primary sources of ancient civilizations. Greece)
Includes bibliographical references and index.
Contents: Gods and goddesses—Greek mythology—The Acropolis and the Parthenon—Temples : places of worship—Religious wisdom—Music and dance—Epic poetry—Theatre and drama—Sculpture—Great thinkers.
ISBN 0-8239-6770-0 (lib. bdg.)—ISBN 0-8239-8938-0 (pbk.)
1. Mythology, Greek—Juvenile literature. 2. Arts, Greek—Juvenile literature. [1. Mythology, Greek. 2. Arts, Greek. 3. Greece—Civilization—To 146 B.C.] I. Title. II. Series.
BL783.A64 2004
292.08—dc21

2002153781

Manufactured in the United States of America

Contents

▲ *Poseidon, Apollo, and Artemis are 3 of the 12 gods worshiped by the ancient Greeks. They are shown here in a carving from the Parthenon, a temple built on Mount Parnassus in Athens to honor Athena.*

Gods and Goddesses

Ancient Greeks worshiped 12 gods and goddesses, as well as many lesser gods. The Greeks believed these beings lived on Mount Olympus, Greece's highest mountain. The Greek people believed that gods and goddesses controlled every part of life. Before hunting, men would pray to Artemis, the goddess of hunting, that they would bring home enough meat for their family. Important events, such as a sea voyage, would begin with an offering to a god, such as Poseidon, the god of the sea. Zeus, the god of the heavens, ruled over everything, including the gods and goddesses. He had taken power from the 12 gods called the Titans, who were the elder gods.

Athena, the goddess of war and wisdom, is shown here dressed for battle. She was the daughter of Zeus, king of the gods. According to Greek myth, she sprang from his head fully grown.

Greek Mythology

Greek myths are a series of well-known stories about the gods and goddesses. These stories are all that is left of ancient Greek religion. The Greeks believed that these stories had been told to humans by the gods, although the stories' true origin is not known. Greek myths told stories of how the universe began, gave some historical facts, taught moral values, and gave meaning to commonly held beliefs and rituals. One myth explains how Athena became the patron of Athens. Both Athena and Poseidon wanted this honor. They had a contest to prove their worthiness to the Athenian people. The people chose Athena, and the city took her name.

In the contest to be chosen as the patron of Athens, Athena caused an olive tree to spring up on the Acropolis. Poseidon caused water to spring forth from the ground. The water was salty, like the sea he ruled.

naos
pronaos
columns

Temples

The ancient Greeks built many temples for their gods. Many towns used their old forts as holy places. Ancient Greeks gathered at these temples to worship their gods. Olympia was the temple at which Zeus was worshiped. At Delphi and Delos, people worshiped Apollo. Every day, people worshiped at shrines in their own courtyards. They said their daily prayers at a family altar, often pouring wine onto the altar as an offering to the gods. On special days, people traveled to the temple in their city-state, where they worshiped outside on the temple grounds.

These temple ruins, dating from the fourth century, are in Turkey, which was then part of Greece. Notice the Ionic columns, which have a scroll design at the top. Inset: *Each temple had a* naos, *a large hall in the temple's center, in which a statue of a god stood. It also had a* pronaos, *an outer room often used as a waiting room. These columns held up a large, sloping roof.*

The Acropolis and the Parthenon

One of the most famous temples built by the Greeks was in Athens. High up on a hill called the Acropolis, which means "high city," was the heart of Athens. It was a large fortress, which served as protection for the Greeks during enemy attacks. The Acropolis was also a place for outdoor festivals. It became the religious center of the city of Athens, too. The Greeks built many temples there in honor of Athena. The largest and most important of these buildings was the Parthenon. It was a beautiful, white building with small windows. Much of the Parthenon still stands today, after almost 2,500 years.

The Acropolis sits at the foot of Mt. Lykabettos and Mt. Penteli in Athens. The Acropolis was built in honor of Athena. ▶

Inset: *The most famous temple at the Acropolis was the Parthenon. Mortar, or cement, was not used in building the temple. Instead holes were made and molten, or melted, lead was inserted. When it hardened, the lead acted similar to a nail or a clamp.*

The Pythia, shown here, was believed to sit on a tripod, or a three-legged seat, in a sleeplike state as Apollo spoke with the visitors through her.

Religious Wisdom

The Greeks believed that the gods talked to them through oracles. Oracles were the people through whom the gods spoke. They were also the places in which the communications took place. The information passed on in answer to the Greeks' questions was also called an oracle. The most famous oracle was located at Delphi, on Mount Parnassus. Here Apollo, the god of the Sun, truth, and music, spoke through a woman called the Pythia. Her answers often came in the form of riddles rather than as direct advice. Some questions were important, but many people went to oracles to ask questions such as, "Should I become a farmer?" and, "Should I get married?"

◀ *Greeks visited the temple at Delphi, shown here, to ask the oracle questions about their future.*

Music and Dance

The arts and religion were often woven together, and they played key roles in the everyday lives of the ancient Greeks. Music was so important in ancient Greece that it was taught in school. Every educated man was expected to know how to play the lyre, a stringed instrument similar to a small harp. Greeks played the lyre to accompany songs and poems. People also played flutes or pipes made of bone or wood. Hymns were played for gods at all public festivals. There were songs for processionals as well as special hymns for weddings, births, and funerals. Dancing occurred at many of these events, too.

Center: *Musicians walk in a procession that is bringing offerings to one of the gods in this painted wooden tablet from 540* B.C.

Nine goddesses, called muses, were the spirits of the arts. People looked to the muses for inspiration in the arts. For example, Terpsichore was the muse of music and dance. Calliope was the muse of epic poetry.

A singer plays the lyre in this ancient Greek sculpture from the eighth century B.C.

Above: *Soldiers fight to save the body of Patroclus, a friend of Achilles, during the Trojan War.*

Epic Poetry

Throughout history, civilizations have tried to pass down their history and legends. One way ancient Greeks did this was through epic poems. These are very long poems that tell stories about heroes. Two of the world's most famous epic poems are *The Iliad* and *The Odyssey*. A blind Greek man named Homer is believed to have told people these poems nearly 3,000 years ago, in the eighth or the ninth century B.C. Though not everything in the stories is true, Homer used them to share some of the early history of Greece. *The Odyssey* is the story of a man named Odysseus and his 10-year voyage home after the defeat of the ancient city of Troy in the Trojan War.

◀ The Iliad *tells the story of the last days of the Trojan War, including the story of a fight between a hero named Achilles and a man named Agamemnon, shown here in this gold mask, who was the leader of the Greek people.*

Theater and Drama

Theater as we know it today began in ancient Greece. Two types of plays in ancient Greece were tragedies and comedies. Tragedies were serious plays about human nature and people's relationships with the gods. Comedies were plays that had happy endings.

Some Greek plays written as many as 3,000 years ago are still read and performed today. For example, *Prometheus Bound* is one of seven surviving plays written by Aeschylus, one of the earliest known writers of Greek tragedy. Aeschylus wrote 83 other plays more than 2,500 years ago, but none of them exist today. Aristophanes wrote more than 40 comic plays, but only 11 still exist.

A chorus of 12 to 15 actors would dress in costumes and large masks, such as the one at right.

The priest of Dionysus, the god of the theater, sat in this throne when he attended the theater.

This Greek theater, now in ruins, could seat 14,000 people when it was in use during the fourth century B.C.

Top: *Phidias carved a scene of the Great Panathenaea, the procession honoring Athena, around the entire Parthenon.* Bottom: *This is the workshop of Phidias.*

Sculpture

Sculpture was an important art form in ancient Greece. Ancient Greek sculptors are famous for sculpting the ideal human form. Those sculptures that have survived the thousands of years since ancient Greek times help people to understand the history and beliefs of the Greeks. Sculptors often created bronze or marble statues of gods and goddesses. Many sculptures were painted with bright colors. Phidias is considered the greatest Greek sculptor. He designed and directed the work on the Parthenon. One of Phidias's most famous sculptures was that of Athena, carved of ivory and gold. Only a few ancient Greek statues exist today. Greeks melted many of their sculptures down so that the bronze could be reused for more useful items such as armor or swords.

Great Thinkers

Philosophy is the study of the basic ideas of knowledge, right and wrong, and reasoning. Socrates, Plato, and Aristotle are the best-known ancient Greek philosophers. These men lived in Athens about 2,500 years ago. Socrates taught by asking questions. He wanted people to think for themselves and to realize how much they did not know. Plato started a school, called the Academy, where he taught students to reason. Aristotle, one of Plato's students, wrote about politics and philosophy. He studied many subjects, such as zoology and physics. Ancient Greek civilization lives on as we continue to study Greek religion, art, and beliefs.

Glossary

city-state (SIH-tee STAYT) An independent state made up of a city and its surrounding areas.

festivals (FES-tih-vulz) Days or special times of rejoicing or feasting.

fortress (FOR-tres) A strong place that can be defended against attacks.

hymns (HIMZ) Songs of praise.

legends (LEH-jendz) Stories, passed down through the years, that cannot be proven.

moral values (MOR-ul VAL-yooz) Beliefs concerning what is wrong and right in human conduct.

patron (PAY-trun) A person who lends their name to a group to show support.

physics (FIH-ziks) The scientific study of matter and energy and their relationships to each other.

processionals (pruh-SESH-nulz) Groups of people moving along in an orderly way for a special purpose or occasion.

rituals (RIH-choo-ulz) Special series of actions done for reasons of faith.

worshiped (WUR-shipt) To have paid great honor and respect to something or someone.

worthiness (WUR-thee-ness) Something that is honorable or important.

zoology (zoh-AH-luh-jee) The study of animals and animal life.

Index

Primary Sources

Cover. Poseidon, Athena, Apollo, and Artemis (left to right). Relief sculpture. Bauron, Greece. Fifth century B.C. **Inset.** Athena confronts Poseidon. Attic black-figure olpe pottery. Painted by Amasis. Sixth century B.C. Musée du Louvre. Paris, France. **Page 4.** Poseidon, Apollo, and Artemis. Relief. East frieze of the Parthenon. Athens, Greece. 440–432 B.C. **Right.** Athena. Marble statue. West frontal of the temple of Aegina, Greece. 490 B.C. National Glyptothek. Munich, Germany. **Page 7.** Athena with her owl in flight and Poseidon with his trident. Detail from a red figure crater. Etruscan vase. Circa 360 B.C. Musée du Louvre. Paris, France. **Page 8.** Temple of Athena. Built by Pitheos at Priene, Turkey, fourth century B.C. **Page 11.** The Acropolis of Athens. Marble. Created by Phidias. Seventh century B.C. **Inset.** The Parthenon. Marble. Created by Phidias. 447–438 B.C. **Page 12. Inset.** Aegeus, king of Athens, consulting the Delphic oracle. Athenian red-figure vase painting. Staatliche Museum. Berlin, Germany. **Page 15. Top.** The Muses. Votive relief. Fifth century B.C. National Archaeological Museum. Athens, Greece. Center. Musicians, sacrificial procession. Pitsa tablet. Painted wood. Found in a cave with two other tablets in Corinthia, Greece. Circa 540 B.C. National Archaeological Museum, Athens, Greece. Bottom. Singer with lyre. Bronze. Geometric period. Eight century B.C. Heraklion, Greece. Heraklion Archaeological Museum. **Page 16.** Fighting over the body of Patroclus in the Trojan War. Black-figure crater. In the style of master Exekias. 530 B.C. Pharsalos, Greece. **Inset.** Gold mask of Agamemnon. Circa 2000 B.C. **Page 19. Top.** Throne of the priest of Dionysus. Marble. Theater of Dionysus. Fourth century B.C. Athens, Greece. Center. Theater at Epidauros. Architect. Polykleitosthe Younger. Fourth century B.C. **Bottom.** Bronze mask. Classical period of Greece. Archaeological Museum Piraeus. **Page 20. Top.** Rearing horse. Elgin marbles. By Phidias. 490–430 B.C. British Museum. **Bottom.** Workshop of Phidias. Originally built to house work on a statue of Zeus for Olympia. 490–430 B.C.

Web Sites

Due to the changing nature of Internet links, PowerKids Press has developed an online list of Web sites related to the subject of this book. This site is updated regularly. Please use this link to access the list: www.powerkidslinks.com/psaciv/artgre/